TRUNGPA

PHOTOGRAPHS

TRUNGPA PHOTOGRAPHS

Naciketas Press
715 E. McPherson
Kirksville, Missouri 63501
2015/2017

ISBN   978-1-936135-16-5 (1-936135-16-7)

Library of Congress Control Number: 2015917134

(Version 1.2)

Published by:
Naciketas Press
715 E. McPherson
Kirksville, Missouri 63501

Available at:
Naciketas Press
715 E. McPherson
Kirksville, Missouri, 63501
Phone: (660) 665-0273
http://www.naciketas-press.com
Email: ndelmoni@gmail.com

Contents

Introduction

Chogyam Turngpa came to Vermont by way of the Surmang Monasteries in Tibet, Dalhousie in India, Oxford in England, Dumfriesshire in Scotland, and Montreal, Quebec. In the spring of 1970, just before going down into Vermont, he gave a talk in Montreal where I heard him speak for the first time. He talked about being a dharma warrior. I wasn't sure what "dharma" was, and I didn't know it had warriors; but the phrase got my attention.

Trungpa settled into a farmhouse on 400 acres in the Vermont hills and named the place Tail of the Tiger. In 1973 I attended a seminar he gave on The Life and Teachings of Naropa. In it he quoted Naropa as having said *Hearing the dharma is like a deer listening to a flute in the forest.* I'd not thought about deer and flutes before, or about hearing the dharma; but the image stuck. I'd been raised a Roman Catholic; for me, listening the Baltimore Catechism had been like sitting in the middle of the freeway hearing a Mack Truck bearing down on you.

At that seminar I got my first good shot of Trungpa. So many people had signed up for the talks that the seminar got moved to the Barnet Town Hall, which also served as a gym and theatre space. Up front, overhead, was a basketball hoop; behind it, on stage, hung a big hand-painted canvas backdrop with a lake, trees, and a castle, bracketed by paintings of ornate stage curtains drawn back. I sat for three days listening to Naropa's difficulties while staring at the hoop, the fake lake, and the guru and got to thinking—maybe life really is an illusion, and maybe this teacher knows the way through, so maybe I should give it a shot to score a connection with him. When the seminar ended, I approached Trungpa and asked if I could remove the front rows of chairs to get a clear shot of him with backdrop and hoop. He agreed. I moved the chairs, walked twenty paces back, aimed my camera, and took one shot. (See page 5.)

Right away I felt regret because what I had really wanted was a close-up. At the next seminar I asked if I could take a close-up and soon found myself being driven to Trungpa's cottage above Tail of the Tiger. As I was being led to Trungpa's room, it occurred to me to panic. I knew NOTHING—not even why I was doing this. I felt fairly certain I was going to get skinned alive. I was shown inside the room; the door closed behind me. Then something strange and delicate occurred. I felt no fear. I looked at Trungpa; he looked at me; neither of us blinked. I moved in close, raised my camera, and squeezed the shutter. Years later it dawned on me that this encounter may well have been what's known as a meeting of the minds. (See page 7.)

Some say I had special access to Trungpa. When I look at my pictures I tend to agree. But whatever access I may have had was granted in silence. There were no discussions of my role as a photographer, there were no contracts, and not once did Trungpa ask to see a single shot. *Basketball* and *Close-up* were the only times I'd asked permission. After them I would just silently stalk my prey, often fretting about being too aggressive. And whenever I'd get a sweet shot, doubts about my approach dissolved. Trungpa was indirectly teaching me how to float like a bee and sting like a butterfly.

I have always liked calling my close-up of Trungpa *The Frog Prince*. You know the story: there is this character who is kind of ugly; then you connect; he turns into a prince. I felt this prince was saying to me: *Welcome. Take it or leave it. It's up to you. Good luck.*

I took it and left it, on and off, for ten years. During that time Trungpa would say, not just to me, but to everybody: *Sit a lot.* I sat a bit. It was hard. I felt bad. It got worse. I became hopeless. Then he'd say, not only to me, but to everyone: *To start on the path you have to be hopeless.* In the darker parts of my psyche, I cheered up.

During a seminar on Marpa Trungpa talked about magic. He said: *Magic is not manipulating reality to make it do whatever you want. Magic is being direct. Not like a needle piercing silk but like a stone-age flint cutting through burlap by crushing the threads.* As a photographer, I knew something about being a needle. But as a high-strung, paranoid, shy person I knew nothing about crushing the burlap between myself and others. This principle of magic connected with something Trungpa told me the one time I asked him about my photographs. It happened at the Rocky Mountain Dharma Center; I'd brought some of my best New York street shots to show him. He looked at them and said: *Don't be afraid to shoot normal.* Right then I realized I'd been cork-screwing reality to make it more dramatic. It took several years before I was able to shoot more simply; when I found my way to it, it turned out to be a lot less work and a lot more fun than shooting with a half-cocked eye through a corkscrew lens.

After ten years around Trungpa I went on to other things for several decades. During that time three seeds were germinating:

- That being hopeless – really hopeless – is not an end, it is a beginning.
- That being direct – really direct – can move mountains, and also molehills.
- It is good to shoot normal; it is also good to just BE normal.

Robert Del Tredici

Naropa University, Nalanda Campus
Sunday, 5 April 2015

Chapter 1:
Tail of the Tiger

Chapter 2:
Karmapa XVI's First Visit to the West

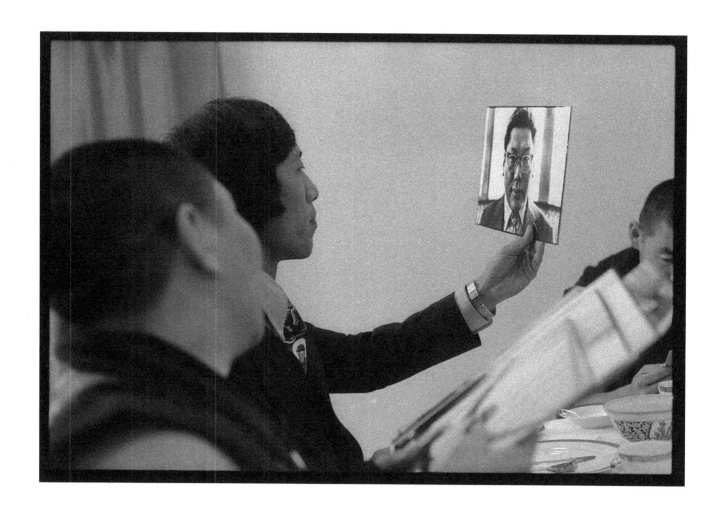

Chapter 3:
The Maitri Center

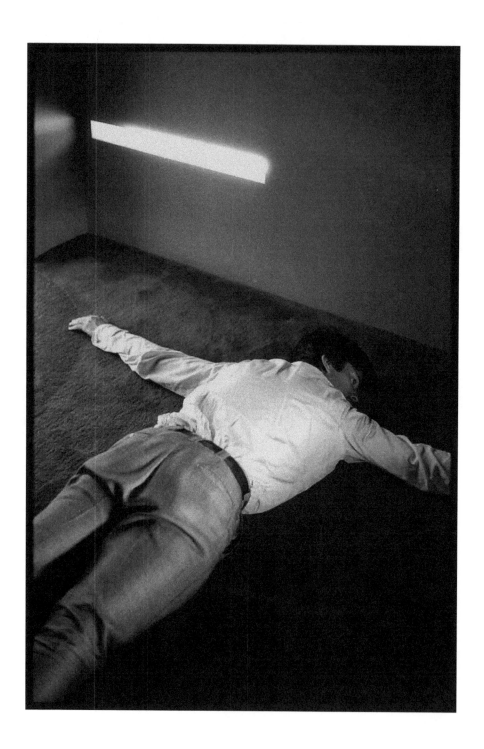

Chapter 4:
Khyentse Rinpoche's First Visit to the West

Chapter 5:
Sitting Meditation

Chapter 6:
Naropa Institute

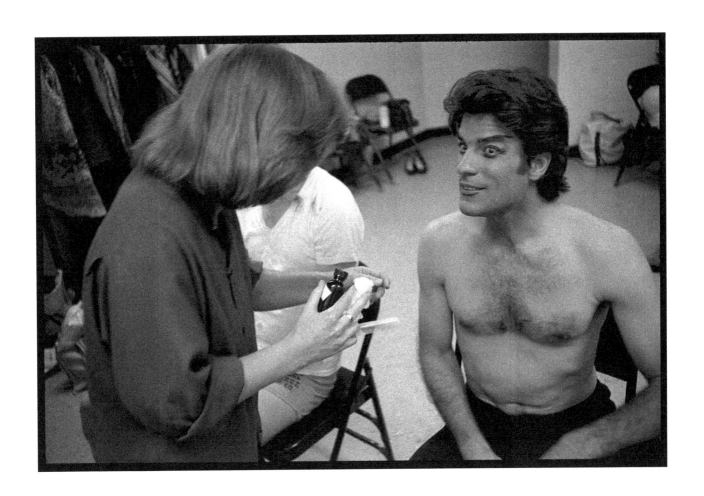

Chapter 7:
Rocky Mountain Dharma Center

Chapter 8:
Poets, Artists, Dancers, and Graduates of Naropa

Chapter 9:
Karmê-Chöling Under Construction

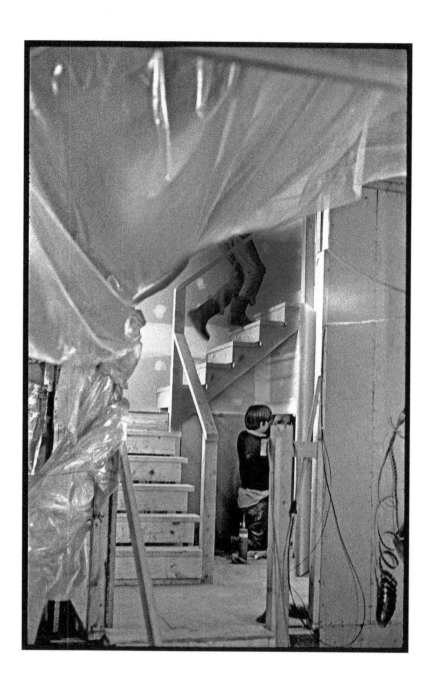

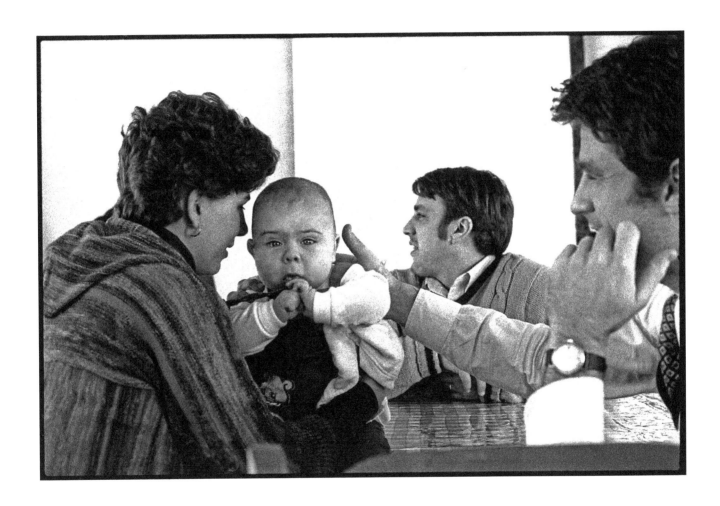

Chapter 10:
Karmapa XVI's Second Visit to the West

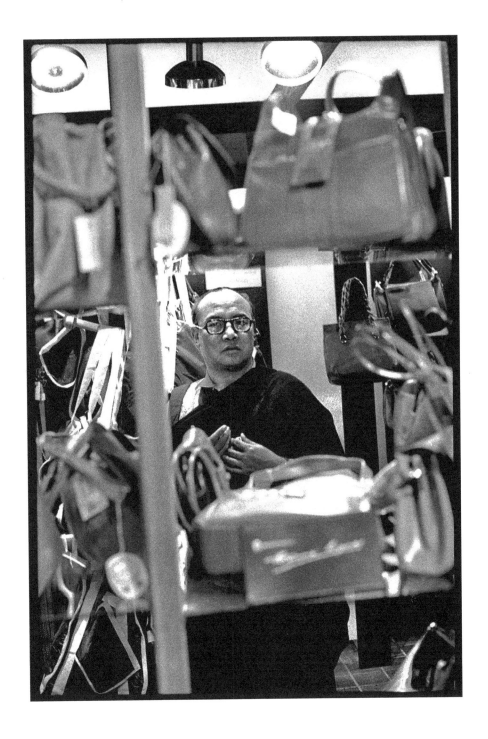

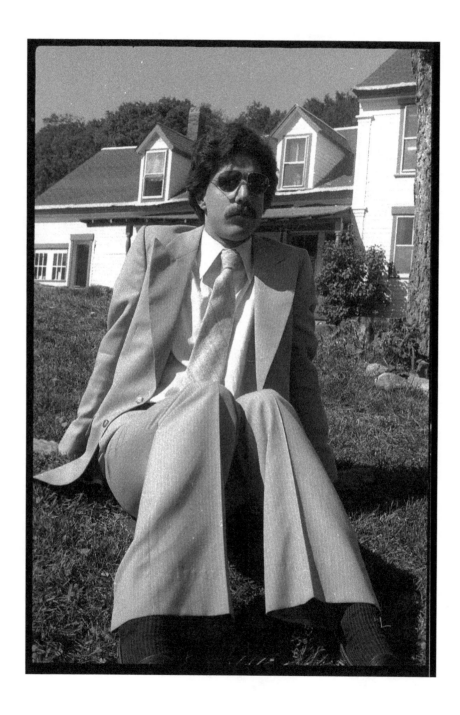

Chapter 11:
Naropa Ikebana

Chapter 12:
Perks Wedding
Golf Day

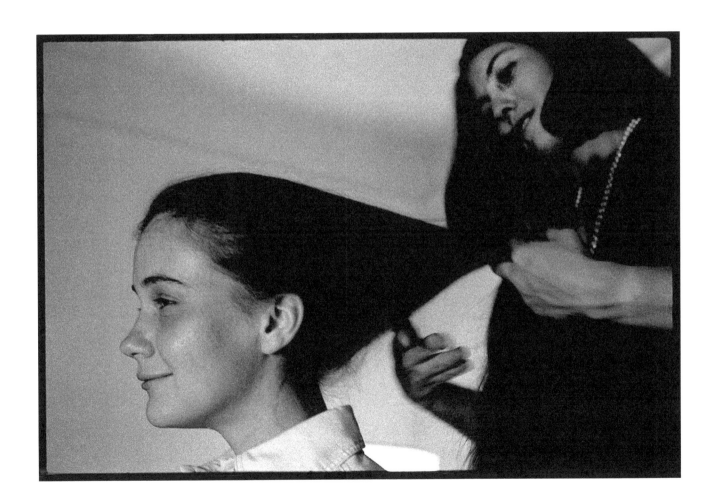

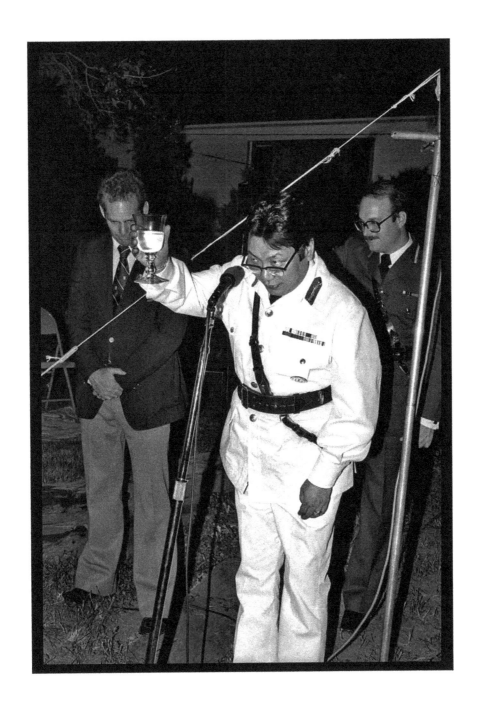

Chapter 13:
Naropa Ikebana (II)

Chapter 14:
Visual Dharma

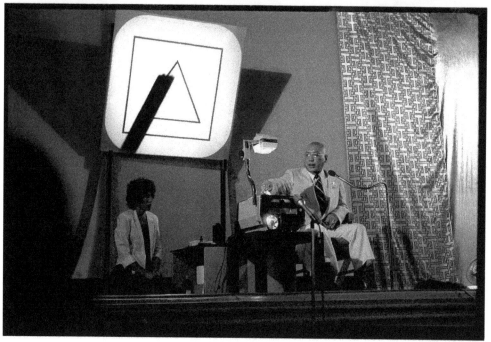

Chapter 15:
With Drala

His Holiness the 17th Gyalwang Karmapa Ogyen Trinley Dorje
(b. 1985) on his third visit to the United States. This picture
was taken soon after Karmapa conducted the Karma Pakshi
Empowerment to a full house in the UPAC Theatre in Kingston,
New York, on Sunday, April 19, 2015.

Robert Del Tredici with Chögyam Trungpa. *Barnet, Vermont, 1973. Photo: Gloria Anuza*

Field Notes
... a work in progress ...

A request: if you can identify any of the people, dates, or places appearing in this book that have so far gone unidentified, please send the information to me at *bobdeltredici@gmail.com* and I will integrate the data into the next version of this book.

With thanks! Bob Del Tredici
www.bobdeltredici.com

1. **The Land.** These 430 acres in the green hills of Vermont were purchased for Chögyam Trungpa on January 7, 1970. Tanya Leontov, Richard Arthure, and Fran Lewis took possession of the property on March 16 of that year, and in the first week of May, 1970, Chögyam Trungpa and his wife Diana arrived. *Photo taken in the early 1970s.*

2. **Main House.** This farm house was once part of a dairy operation; it became the early headquarters for Chögyam Trungpa, who named the house and land Tail of the Tiger. Behind the trees, new structures are visible; they were built in the mid-1970s when Tail of the Tiger was re-named Karmê-Chöling. *369 Patneaude Lane, Barnet, Vermont, mid-1970s.*

3. **Chögyam Trungpa Rinpoche** was a meditation master, teacher, and artist. His family name was Mupgo. One of his *dharma* names was Chökyi Gyatso ("Ocean of Dharma").

He was the holder of two Tibetan Buddhist lineages: the Kagyu lineage (also referred to as The Practicing Lineage,

The Whispered Lineage, and The Mishap Lineage) associated with the Mahamudra tradition of Buddhism; and the Nyingma lineage (also called the Ancient School), associated with the Maha-ati tradition and based on the teachings that Padmasambhava brought from India to Tibet in the eighth century. Trungpa was recognized soon after his birth as the eleventh Trungpa Tulku. In Tibet he was the supreme abbot of the Surmang Monasteries. He fled the Chinese in Tibet and became a pivotal figure in bringing Tibetan Buddhism to the West. He coined the terms "crazy wisdom" and "spiritual materialism." *Tail of the Tiger, early 1970s.*

4. **Flag One** was designed by Trungpa in 1972 and sewn by Sara Kapp. This was Trungpa's first dharma banner. In the center of the flag is a circle surrounding the Eternal Knot, also referred to as The Knot of Meditation; around it are pennant ribbons whose colors are meant to blend the banner with the environment: the blue ribbon represents sky; the white ribbon stands for clouds; orange is for the sun; yellow is for more sunshine; purple stands for mountains; green stands for grass. *Tail of the Tiger, 1973.*

5. **Basketball.** This picture was taken at the end of the 3-day seminar on The Life and Teachings of Naropa, Part II. High enrollment resulted in the seminar's being relocated from Tail of the Tiger to the nearby Barnet Town Hall and gym. *Barnet, Vermont, 1973.*

7. **Close-Up.** *Chögyam Trungpa in his cottage above Tail of the Tiger, 1973.*

8. **Hippy and Buddha.** Trungpa arrived in the West in 1970 at a time when America's hippy culture was still much in evidence. *Tail of the Tiger, early 1970s.*

9. **Writing Refuge Names (part 1).** The first level of a student's commitment to Buddhism expresses itself in the refuge vow; when students take refuge in the Buddha, the Dharma, and the Sangha, they receive a protection cord and a refuge name that emphasizes the student's enlightened potential. *In the dining room of Trungpa's cottage above Tail of the Tiger, early 1970s.*

10. **Gesar Mugpo,** Trungpa's son, with his mother Diana. *Tail of the Tiger, early 1970s.*

11. **Sakyong Gong.** A young Sakyong Mipham at *Tail of the Tiger, mid-1970s.*

12. **Up from the Land.** *Tail of the Tiger, early 1970s.*

13. **Entering the Main House.** *Tail of the Tiger, early 1970s.*

14. **Cook.** Mary Spoto helps prepare dinner for seminar attendees. *Tail of the Tiger, early 1970s.*

15. **Kitchen Hand.** *Tail of the Tiger, early 1970s.*

16. **Kitchen Workers.** *Tail of the Tiger, mid-1970s.*

17. **Sam and Hazel Bercholz** with their first child Sara. In 1969 Sam founded Shambhala Publications with Michael Fagan in Berkeley, California. Its first book was Trungpa's *Meditation in Action* (1969). In 1973 Shambhala published *Cutting Through Spiritual Materialsm.* At last count, Shambhala has published 21 Trungpa titles. *Tail of the Tiger, early 1970s.*

18. **Writing Refuge Names (part 2).** Robin Kornman (top); Jan Watson (middle); Larry Marmelstein. *In the dining room of Trungpa's cottage above Tail of the Tiger, early 1970s.*

19. **Winter Light.** *Trungpa at his cottage above Karmê-Chöling, mid-1970s.*

20. **Summer Discussions.** *Karmê-Chöling, mid-1970s.*

21. **Poised.** *Karmê-Chöling, mid-1970s.*

23. **His Holiness the XVI Gyalwa Karmapa, Ranjung Khyabdak Rigpe Dorje (1924-1981), Head of the Karma-Kagyu Lineage, enters Karmê-Chöling.** Karl Springer leads the way; Bill McKeever is on Karmapa's left. Inside, Karmapa's translator Achi Tsepal stands on the rug by the door. His Holiness is often referred to as a Dharma King. In Trungpa's book *The Mishap Lineage* (Shambhala Books, 2009), Trungpa tells how Karmapa had a vision that guided monks to the Kham region of Tibet to find and identify the newly born Chökyi Gyatso as the reincarnation of the tenth Trungpa Tulku. At eighteen months, the child was enthroned by Karmapa as the eleventh Trungpa Tulku. On His Holiness' first visit to Vermont, Karmapa renamed Tail of the Tiger "Karme-Cho-Kyi-Ling," or Karmê-Chöling ("Dharma Place of the Karma Kagyu"). *Photo taken on Karmapa's second visit to the West in 1976.*

24. **Tsultim Namgyal,** one of the monks traveling with Karmapa during Karmapa's first visit to the West. *Karmê-Chöling, 1974.*

25. **Shrine Room Make-over.** Fran Davis at left. Behind Karmapa, large portraits of the Lohan sculptures on the shrine room wall installed in anticipation of Karmapa's visit. *Karmê-Chöling, September, 1974.*

26. **Translator Achi Tsepal Studies Trungpa Portrait.** *Karmê-Chöling, September, 1974.*

27. **Karmapa Enthusiasm.** Monk Jomgon Kongtrul III at right. *Karmê-Chöling, 1974.*

28. **Karmapa Ponders.** Karmapa's first visit to the West in 1974 included stops in London, New York, and Long Island before he arrived at Tail of the Tiger, which he renamed Karmê-Chöling. After Vermont he traveled to Massachusetts, Michigan, and Colorado. In early October, 1974, he asked to be driven to the Hopi Second Mesa in Arizona where he met Chief Ned, who told Karmapa that no rain had fallen in 75 days. Karmapa prayed for the Chief; within an hour there was a great rainstorm (described by eye-witness Steve Roth on *Kagyu.org*). Karmapa also visited New Mexico, California, British Columbia, Toronto, and Montreal. During his 1974 visit Karmapa empowered Chögyam Trungpa as "Vajra Holder and Possessor of the Victory Banner of the Practice Lineage of the Karma Kagyu." (This proclamation can be seen in Garuda IV, 1976.) On his way back to India Karmapa visited Scotland, Norway, Sweden, Denmark, Holland, West Germany, and France. *Karmê-Chöling, 1974.*

29. **The Evening Before Trungpa Goes On One-Year Retreat in Charlemont, Massachusetts.** *Karmê-Chöling, December, 1977.*

30. **Trungpa Under a Photo of his Root Guru Jomgon Kongtrul of Shechen (1902-1952).** When the young Trungpa met and studied with Jomgon Kongturl at his monastery in Sechen, everything changed. "He joked around, he was very jolly, and he was very kind and soft and insightful. Sometimes he didn't even sit upright," Trungpa says of his root guru, adding, "he was the real embodiment of sanity." (*The Mishap Lineage*, edited by Carolyn Gimian, Shambhala Publications, 2009, page 68-9). Jomgon Kongtrul of Sechen was one of several incarnations of Jomgon Kongtrul the Great (1813-1899) who championed an ecumenical approach to all Buddhist schools of thought. He helped compile the teachings of the Sakya, Kagyu, Geluk, and Nyingma lineages. Jomgon Kongtrul of Sechen followed this tradition, as did Chögyam Trungpa. Only two photographs of Jomgon Kongtrul of Sechen are known to exist. The picture above Trungpa here was taken in a Chinese photo studio. The second portrait, below, was taken by Chögyam Trungpa. With Jan Watston. *Mid-1970s, Karmê-Chöling.*

Jomgon Kongtrul of Sechen. *Photo by Chögyam Trungpa.*

31. **Monk Yonten with Tangerine.** Yonten helped Trungpa escape from the Communist Chinese in Tibet in 1959. At the age of 19, with a price on his head, Trungpa led an escape party of several hundred Tibetans for ten months through near-arctic conditions towards India. They were under continual threat of discovery by Chinese troops. He took evasive action over 18,000 foot peaks and made a mid-winter

climb across the Himalayas. At one point food was in such short supply they boiled leather and ate it. About 50 Tibetans completed the escape.

At right, Fred Ferraris stands next to Monk Ugyen-Shenpen, a member of the Nalanda Translation Committee. The calligraphy on the wall by Trungpa says "*Always meditate on that which is most difficult. If you do not start right away, the moment a difficulty arises, it is very hard to overcome it.*" This is Trungpa's commentary on the 49th Slogan of Atisha Dipankara, the 11th century teacher of the Kadam school. Slogan 49 (out of 59) is entitled "*Always meditate on whatever provokes resentment.*" This calligraphy can be found in *The Profound Treasury of the Ocean of Dharma, Vol. 2, The Bodhisattva Path of Wisdom and Compassion*, page 362 (edited by Judith Lief, Shambhala Books, 2013). *Photo: Karmê-Chöling, during Khyentse Rinpoche's visit to Vermont, 1976.*

32. "*Jolly Good Luck*" was a phrase Trungpa used the night before he went into one-year retreat in Charlemont, MA. In his will, Trungpa included a final poem that used this same phrase. The sleeve in the upper right of this picture belongs to Steve Jewell. The sleeve in the lower left of the picture belongs to Madeleine Korman, mother of Ellen Korman, who married Steve Mains on this day at *Karmê-Chöling, February 26 or 27, 1977.*

33. **The Road to Karmê-Chöling** *on Patneaude Lane, Barnet, Vermont, 1977.*

35. **Entrance to the Maitri Center.** Inspired by Suzuki Roshi, Trungpa developed the idea for the Maitri Center in 1973 at Snow Lion in Jackson Hole, Wyoming. Trungpa created the Maitri Space Awareness rooms and practices to enhance and clarify the experience of the energies of the five Buddha families. *With Mary Ann Flood's dog Gypsy. Wingdale, New York, 1976.*

36. **Striking the Gong.** Joan Springer ends a meditation session in the Maitri Community Room. The banner in the slanted sunlight "Maitri." *Meditation Building, Maitri Center, Wingdale, New York, 1977.*

37. **Building with the Five Buddha Family Rooms.** On the wall closest to the viewer the narrow Vajra window slits are visible. At the end of the porch is the round Ratna window. On the roof is the top end of the Karma tunnel window. The qualities of the five Buddha Families in the captions on pages 38 to 42 are based on discussions with Maitri directors and Trungpa's descriptions in the chapter on Tantra in *Cutting Through Spiritual Materialism*. *Maitri Center, Wingdale, New York, 1977.*

38. **The Vajra Room** is deep blue, with narrow slits for windows. The posture in this room is lying face down, turned away from the window slits. Vajra energy includes anger, aggression, sharpness, precision; it is associated with water, winter, dawn, white, and the East. Its Karma energy: Pacifying. It can transmute into the luminosity of Mirror-like Wisdom. James Yensan holds the pose. *Maitri Center, 1977.*

39. **The Karma Room**, first painted deep green, was redone by Trungpa in pale mint, like oxidized copper. The posture in this room is lying on the back in a slightly spread-eagle position, looking up into a tunnel-like window. Karma energy includes competition, paranoia, envy, efficiency. It is associated with wind, summer, night, and the North. Its Karma energy: Destroying. It can transmute into the Wisdom of All-Accomplishing Action. *Maitri Center, 1977.*

40. **The Ratna Room** was first painted daffodil yellow then redone by Trungpa in deep gold; he also had the window enlarged. The posture is lying face up, spread-eagle, facing the window. Ratna energy is associated with pride and solidity, mountains, hills, autumn, mid-morning, and the South. Its Karma energy: Enriching. It can transmute into the All-pervading Wisdom of Equanimity. James Yensan holds the pose. *Maitri Center, 1977.*

41. **The Suzuki Roshi Rock** was so named because of a calligraphy Trungpa made after Suzuki Roshi died on December 4, 1971: "A solitary rock is majestic. In Memory of Suzuki Roshi. Chögyam." The rock was selected by Kobun Chino Roshi. Joe Caradona pulled it out of the river with a backhoe. The calligraphy is reproduced in the *Garuda* magazine entitled "Working with Negativity." *Maitri Center, 1977.*

42. **The Padma Room.** The original red of this room Trungpa made more luminous, and he enlarged and lowered the windows. The posture is lying on the right side, facing the windows with knees drawn up, the head on the right arm, the

left arm on the body. Padma includes self and other, perception, desire, seduction, hospitality, art. It is associated with fire, early spring, meadows, sunset, and the West. Its Karma energy: Magnetizing. It can transmute into Discriminating-Awareness Wisdom. *Maitri Center, 1977.*

43. **Organic Vegetable Garden** with Suzanne Townsend. *Maitri Center, 1976.*

44. **On Maitri Ground**. Jim Yensan with Mary Ann Flood and her dog Gypsy. *Maitri Center, 1976.*

Jane Carpenter Cohn teaches the Maitri practice at Naropa. For the Maitri section of photographs in the exhibit on Trungpa Rinpoche at Naropa's Nalanda campus (January 2015), she provided this description of the Maitri practice:

Maitri

Jane Carpenter Cohn

Chögyam Trungpa Rinpoche's design of the Maitri Space Awareness rooms was inspired by conversation with Shunryu Suzuki Roshi in May, 1971 at the San Francisco Zen Center. The Maitri rooms were designed to meet the needs of people who were unable to do the sitting practice of meditation due to extreme psychological and emotional states of mind. This was just the beginning in the discovery of the potency and power of the rooms to support creativity, opening sense perceptions, and emotional intelligence in the process of uncovering a broader spectrum of human experience.

This method of inquiry is based on the ancient mandala principle as founded in Tibetan Vajrayana Buddhism. This principle is a comprehensive understanding and experience of the entire universe, which includes all states of mind. The emotions are seen as expressions of mind that can give rise to a sense of ease, relaxation and sanity or create disturbance in the form of negative emotions and fixations. In short, it is the same mind that one is experiencing. Through

one lens we experience that mind as sanity and through the other dis-ease, a sense of being separate from ourselves and the world.

Though Maitri Space Awareness practice is directly based on Vajrayana Buddhist ritual practices, Rinpoche dismantled the religious and cultural trappings to reveal its essence. This allows us to step into the mandala of our own mind and world, without the protection and confusion of an esoteric cover, by passing the potential for spiritual materialism. Without any cultural entrapments, we dive into the rawness of life, an unfiltered reality. No hiding in the Maitri rooms, just mind, body and space!

The practice consists of being open to everything that arises in our mind and body while being in a particular posture in a particular colored room: white, blue, yellow, red and green.

The rooms are a mirror of our multifaceted mind that we often choose to ignore. It seems much easier to see ourselves in a limited way, to be comfortable. The Maitri rooms invite us to come out in all of our colors. They allow us to say yes to arts of ourselves that feel foreign or dormant and to draw on their richness and expression with the ground of openness and kindness. Through openness and loving-kindness towards one's own confusion, one discovers the underlying wisdom.

I began the practice in 1975 at the Naropa Institute summer session. I am not sure how far I would have gone with just sitting still on the cushion without the invitation to know my mind and emotions with such accuracy. How was it that this ancient tradition could describe my daily perceptions with such precision? It was not easy, but the sense that this world was more than my narrow lens was fascinating as well as exposing.

I am personally astounded and humbled each semester by the power of this practice. Students come on skeptical and giggly, leaving the semester not only with a deeper and broader understanding of themselves but with compassion for those who previously seemed foreign and difficult.

45. **Karmê-Chöling Gold Leaf Team.** After completing his one-year retreat in Charlemont, Massachusetts, Trungpa met with the students who had just spent one year gold-leafing the installation behind them. Second from left: Polly Monner; third from left: Ann Shaftel; fourth from left: Bart Mendel; fifth from left: Ann McClellan; sixth: Marilyn Wegener; seventh: Laura Jane Zimmer-Reed; eighth: Tamara Wieder; far right: Richard John. *Shrine Room, Karmê-Chöling, December 1978.*

46. **People of the Porch.** Behind the white pillar, center: Gloria Anuza. Front group: fourth person from left: Karen Wilding; fifth person: Susan Dreier; ninth person (at end): June Krow. *Tail of the Tiger, early 1970s.*

47. **Red Carpet** for His Holiness Dilgo Khyentse Rinpoche (1910-1991), meditation master and head of the Nyingma/Maha Ati school (1987-1991), visiting the West for the first time. The word "Khyentse" combines two Tibetan words: *khyen*, meaning wisdom, and *tse*, meaning compassion. He is accompanied by monks that include, far left, Yonten; behind him, Lama Ugyen-Shenpen of the Nalanda Translation Committee; Khyentse holds the forearm of his attendant and translator Tulku Pema Wangyal. Directly behind Khyentse is Bhagvan Dass; behind him is Hector McLean. Khyentse spent nearly three months in the USA; he visited Vermont, Boulder, New Mexico, and the San Francisco Bay Area. *Karmê-Chöling, spring of 1978.*

49. **"Mr. Universe" greets the photographer.** Students would sometimes refer to Khyentse Rinpoche as "Mr. Universe" out of appreciation for the scope and depth of his teachings. Khyentse, a champion of the non-sectarian approach to spirituality, was a lineage holder of all four schools of Tibetan Buddhism. *Karmê-Chöling, 1978.*

50. **Khyentse Rinpoche Coaches his Grandson Sechen Rabjum, Tulku.** Rabjum grew up to become his grandfather's spiritual heir. *Karmê-Chöling, 1978.*

51. **Shechen Rabjam** studies on his own. *Karmê-Chöling, 1976.*

52. **Hand-to-Brow Transmission.** In the years that followed, Khyentse appointed Shechen Rabjam the abbot of the Shechen Tennyi Dargye Ling monastery in Bodhnath, Nepal. Khyentse founded the monastery in 1984, making it his main seat. Today the monastery under Shechen Rabjam supports over 400 monks. *Karmê-Chöling, 1976.*

53. **Grandfather, Grandson.** *Karmê-Chöling, 1976.*

54. **Khyentse Reading Scriptures.** *Karmê-Chöling, 1976.*

55. **Khyentse with Trungpa.** Khyentse was one of the teachers of Chögyam Trungpa as well as of Karmapa XVI. In addition, he was the Dalai Lama's principal teacher in the Nyingma and Dzogchen traditions. He was also the spiritual advisor to the royal family of Bhutan. *Karmê-Chöling, 1976.*

56. **Mystery Mudra.** Some say Khyentse's hand gestures here represent Tibetan dance moves. Others quip that he may be asking where his thermos is. I feel these gestures are a *mudra*; but if so, which *mudra* are they? *Karmê-Chöling, 1976.*

57. **Tea Break.** *Karmê-Chöling, 1976.*

58. **Flatbed Express.** Khyentse Rinpoche and three of his monks are borne over winter terrain to a retreat hut above the Karmê-Chöling main building. Right: Bill McKeever; center: Jan Watson. Monk to the right of Jan Watson: Lama Ugyen-Shenpen of the Nalanda Translation Committee; monk to the left of Jan: Tulku Pema Wangyal; monk in front of Khyentse: Yonten. *Karmê-Chöling, March 1976.*

59. **Khyentse Crossing Rivulet en Route to Hut.** The tractor pulling the flatbed is driven by Hector McLean. *Karmê-Chöling, 1976.*

60. **Sangha Converging on Retreat Hut.** *Karmê-Chöling, 1976.*

61. **Khyentse Blesses the Stream Hut.** This retreat hut, called "the Stream Hut," was among the first three 8' x 8' retreat huts built at Karmê-Chöling. Khyentse's arrival surprised the monk Tsultim in retreat there; he had no idea such a visitation had been scheduled for that morning. *Karmê-Chöling, 1976.*

63. **Spiegel Under Buddha**: How not to do sitting meditation. In the Smoking Room, under a painting of the Buddha by Jack Niland, Eric Spiegel takes a break. *Tail of the Tiger, July, 1973. See also page 172.*

64. **Sitter under Lohan,** *Karmê-Chöling, 1977.*

65. **"You don't say"** was a phrase Trungpa used often. The flip-side of this phrase was a phrase Trungpa used even more often: "Just do it." *Tail of the Tiger, 1973.*

66. **Hauling Zabutons Under Lohans.** Trungpa had large portraits of the Lohans installed in the Shrine Room in anticipation of Karmapa's first visit. Zabutons by Samadhi Cushions, Inc. *Shrine Room, Karmê-Chöling, 1974.*

67. **Into Retreat.** Barry Mendel drives Betty Lees with her retreat supplies up steep terrain above Karmê-Chöling's main building to the site of the hut where she will do her first retreat. Her retreat lasted 9 days. *Karmê-Chöling, September, 1978.*

68. **Under the Big Top.** Summer seminar at *Karmê-Chöling, mid-1970s.*

69. **On Solid Ground.** *Karmê-Chöling, mid-1970s.*

71. **Fan Man.** After his one-year retreat in Charlemont in 1977, Trungpa introduced the Shambhala teachings and stepped up his teachings on Dharma Art. *Karma-Dzong, Boulder, 1978.*

72. **Dharma Yodel.** Allen Ginsberg (1926-1997) with his partner the poet Peter Orlovsky (1933-2010) make music at Naropa. Ginsberg, with Anne Waldman, John Cage, and Diane di Prima, founded Naropa's Jack Kerouac School of Disembodied Poetics in 1974, in time for Naropa's first summer session. Ginsberg first met Trungpa serendipitously in a shared cab-ride in Manhattan. *Naropa, first summer session, 1974.*

73. **Drum Lesson (1)** with Sara Coleman. The infant's name is Clancy, the child of Alice Nowell. *Naropa, first summer session, 1974.*

74. **Drum Lesson (2)** with Sara Coleman. In background, leaning left: Jack Niland. *Naropa, first summer session, 1974.*

76. **Jazz Drummer Jerry Granelli** started the Creative Music Program at Naropa in the mid-1970s. In the mid-1960s he performed with the Vince Guaraldi Trio for *A Charlie Brown Christmas*; he was a session musician for Sly Stone; and he has played with the Kingston Trio and the Grateful Dead, among others. Gene Krupka and Charlie Parker were decisive musical influences. He met Trungpa in the 1970s and moved to Boulder to develop the music program at Naropa. *Naropa, mid-1970s.*

75. **Object Arrangement,** a Visual Dharma class led by Jack Niland (far right, center) at Naropa. Upper left: Herb Elesky; third person over, in front of banner: Avilda Moses; fourth person: John Steinbeck, Jr. (seated); center: Peter Goldfarb. Above John Steinbeck Jr., standing: Nancy Craig. Directly below her, seated: Susan Srier. Below Susan, half-hidden by Jack Niland: Hazel Bercholtz. Woman doing arrangement: Marlo Brooks. Bottom center, with back to camera, calligrapher Barbara Bash. *On the Rainbow Rug in the "Bus Terminal" main room, Naropa, late 70s.*

In 1973 Trungpa expanded his world with the first seminary at the Snow Lion Inn in Jackson Hole, Wyoming; he acquired the Hotel for a year and asked Jack Niland to decorate the whole building with flags and banners in a variety of sizes to enhance the space as a Buddhist seminary in the off-season, from September to November; and, during the tourist season, to present clients with colorful Himalayan décor. When Jack asked Trungpa how he would pay for the project, Trungpa said *"You have to pay for it. We have no money."*

"How will I pay for it?" Jack asked.

"I will give you a dharma art task: you will turn Sara into a top model. But you have to follow my instructions exactly." Jack's partner Sara had been trying for years to become a professional model and given up on it. Trungpa told Jack to get rid of all of Sara's hippy clothes and throw away all her fashion photos. Then he asked them to pick a designer they both liked, someone with clarity and presence, and find an outfit for Sara that would personify this designer. They chose fashion-star Valentino; he was big in Italy but little known in the US. Jack bought Sara a black bell-bottom jumpsuit in Filene's Basement for $10. Trungpa then told Jack to look objectively at Sara *"the way you'd look at a seashell"* and do whatever it took to make her go with the outfit to express the essence of the designer. Jack cut Sara's hair very short, dyed it

maroon like a monk's robe, and gave her ancient Egyptian eye make-up. Then they chanced to learn that Valentino would be coming to the US for the first time, and in New York City he would be holding an open call for models. At the event Sara walked up to Valentino and said, "*I'm your new muse. And I'm 18.*" (She was 27.) He said "*OK! OK!*" and invited her to his villa in Capri. Within a week he had designed a new line of clothes inspired by her.

That is how Sara became a top model, and she made big money at it for 17 years. Jack set up a loft studio over 18th and Broadway in New York and silk-screened everything needed for The Snow Lion Inn. That next year saw the opening of Naropa, with 2000 students attending the first session; Jack made flags and banners to celebrate and decorate the event. That same year Trungpa invited His Holiness Karmapa XVI to visit the US for the first time. Karmapa was the chief lineage holder of the Kagyu tradition, a teacher of Trungpa's, and the one who identified Trungpa at birth. Jack moved his Banner Studio to Boulder and enhanced Karmapa ("the Dharma King")'s presence with new backdrops, banners, and flags. In Boulder he continued to mass-produce satin graphics for seminars, shrines, and dharma events for Trungpa's ever-expanding world and for dharma centers across the country.

Jack Niland (mid-1970s) — Sara Kapp (mid-1970s)

77. Make-up for Frank Berliner as Nanki-Poo in The Mikado. *Naropa, Longmont, June 28, 1979.*

78. Make-up for Peter Goldfarb as the Mikado. *Naropa, Longmont, June 28, 1979.*

79. Peter Goldfarb as The Mikado. Peter Goldfarb proposed and directed Gilbert and Sullivan's *The Mikado* for Regent Osel Tendzin's 36th birthday on June 28, 1979. Chögyam Trungpa contributed ideas for sets and costumes; they were executed by Maurice McClelland. The Nalanda Players performed the musical three times in the Vance Brand Theater in Longmont, a suburb of Boulder. Goldfarb directed an additional performance for a video, now a dvd, entitled *The Mikado by the Nalanda Players. Naropa, Longmont. June 28, 1979.*

81. Cast of The Mikado. *Naropa, Longmont, June 30, 1979.*

DRAMATIS PERSONAE

Ko-Ko — Lord High Executioner of Titipu .... Michael Klarreich
Pooh-Bah — Lord High Everything Else .... Steven Hirsch
Pish-Tush — A Noble Lord .... Roland Cohen
Nanki-Poo — The Mikado's son, disguised as a wandering minstrel, and in love with Yum-Yum .... Frank Berliner

Yum-Yum ⎫ .... Chandrika Austin Fernandez
Pitti-Sing ⎬ Three wards of Ko-Ko .... Rayna Jacobsen
Peep-Bo ⎭ .... Jacqueline Trump
Katisha — An Elderly Lady, in love with Nanki-Poo ..... Betty Kopit
The Mikado of Japan .... Peter Goldfarb

Chorus of Noblemen and Villagers: Peter Allen, Richard Assaly, Peter Barbieri, Joe Caradonna, James Elliot, Charles Galaitis, Neal Greenberg, Newcomb Greenleaf, Michael Miller, Tom Pathe, Joe Puleo, Richard Rahn, George Ramsey, Michael Reshetnik, Michael Schmidt, Jim Torbert, Mark Turnoy, Bruce Wauchope, Paul Wegener, Andrew Weiner

Chorus of Schoolgirls: Helen Berliner, Jolie Bernstein, Julie Dubose, Suzanne Furman, Molly Greacen, Margot Iseman, Lindy King, Lisa Kipnes, Lee Kirkland, Poppy Koch, Marcy Krichels, Kathy McCullough, Diane Moburg, Grace Morgan, Eve Reshetnik, Patty Ronca, Edie Smith, Barbara Stankiewicz, Marilyn Wegener

Guards: Howard Klein, Fleet Maull, Henry Schaeffner, Paul Susnis, Blake Thomson

Orchestra: *1st Violins:* Paula Harvey, Marsha Johnson; *2nd Violins:* Kathy Rinhart, Natalie Gray; *Violas:* Dianne Olson, Sonya Reberg; *Celli:* John Ramsey, Cathy Batka; *Bass:* Terry Sines; *Flutes:* Phyllis Stanard, Mary Goble; *Oboe:* Jack Bartow; *Clarinets:* Richard Johnson, Shirley Kassinger; *Bassoon:* Jim Cochrane; *Trumpets:* Linda Carter, John Hoffman; *Horns:* Drew Kearns, David Gasser; *Trombone:* John van Brodt; *Percussion:* Dana Axelson.

PRODUCTION STAFF

Assistant to the Producer:
Kristine Ellis
Production Assistant:
Jerry Granelli, Pam Schmidt
Assistant to the Director:
Matthew Rubin
Assistant to the Musical Director:
Pat Bandak
Stage Managers:
Marv Ross, Ed Roth
Technical Directors:
Maurice McClelland, Bruce Resnicoff
Set Construction:
Bruce Resnicoff, Joe Caradonna
Set Painting:
Daniel Johnson, Randy Hester
David Mann
Sound Technicians:
Bruce Wauchope, Stefan Carmine
Dresser:
Michelle De Raismes
Hair Design:
Aiko Sturdevant, Stephen/Aida
Make-Up:
Aiko Sturdevant, Robin Gaylord
Kelly
Property Mistress:
Frances Harwood
Variety Worker:
Suzanne Furman
Production Secretary:
Rita Onuferko
Acting Advisors:
Lee Worley, Maggie Donaghy

Publicity Director:
Robert Morehouse
Media Co-ordinator:
Miriam Arguelles
Longmont Liaisons:
Giannina Hughes, Douglass Hughes
Personal Appearances:
Mary Smith
Radio-Television:
Jim Hoagland
Press:
Kathy McCullough

Playbill Editor:
Peter W. Livingston
Playbill Advertising:
Mary Newton
Playbill Design/Production:
Vermilion Graphics
Poster Design:
Gina Janowitz
Logo Design:
Barbara Bash
Photographer:
Blair Hansen

Business Consultant:
David Darwent
Ticket Sales:
Dee Dee Crane, Bonnie Hurst
Steven Carter
Head Usher:
Tom Brown
Ushers:
The Padma Committee
Vance Brand Auditorium Technicians:
Mrs. Johanna Ramsey, Gary Helmers

Two pages from the original 1979 Mikado program.

82. Tibetan Thangka Master Tendzin Rongae taught *thangka* painting at Naropa. He sits with his grandson Tsering Rongae, son of Noedup Rongae. *Naropa, mid-1970s.*

83. Glen Eddy (1941-2006) taught *thangka* painting at Naropa's first summer session. He was one of the first westerners to become fully trained in traditional Tibetan *thangka*

painting. His teachers included Tarthang Tulku, Dudjom Rinpoche, Gyaltrul Rinpoche, and Chögyam Trungpa Rinpoche. He made his own paints from minerals he collected according to centuries-old guidelines. His spare, elegant line drawings are included in Trungpa's *Cutting Through Spiritual Materialism*, *The Myth of Freedom*, and *The Dawn of Tantra*. At the time of his death in Argentina in 2006 he was working on *The Treasury of Luminous Manifestation*, a primer he said he was composing for *thangka* painters 100 years from now. *First summer session, Naropa 1974. (tsetso.blogspot.ca/2006/04/glen-eddy)*

85. **Main Tent, Rocky Mountain Dharma Center.** In early Tibet, at the time of the first Trungpas, there were few monasteries; tent culture was the preferred mode of manifesting monastic dharma. Tent encampments as elaborate as whole small cities would spring up in empty valleys overnight; teachings and rituals would be given; a day later the encampment would be gone. Trungpa says the concept was partly borrowed from Ghenghis Khan and Mongolian culture. Tent culture flourished in Tibet from the 14th to 16th centuries. Traces of Tibetan tent culture were in evidence at the Rocky Mountain Dharma Center. *Rocky Mountain Dharma Center, northern Colorado, mid-1970s.*

86. **Breakfast Under Marpa Point.** The Rocky Mountain Dharma Center was founded by Chögyam Trungpa in 1971. Its 600 acres were initially "tamed" by a group of unconventional practitioners who called themselves "the Pygmies." Today the site has been named The Shambhala Mountain Center. One year after Trungpa's death, the building of a memorial *stūpa* ("the Great Stupa of Dharmakaya") began in his honor. It took 13 years to complete. It can be found near Marpa Point in a meadow at the upper end of the land. *Red Feather Lakes, near Fort Collins, northern Colorado, mid-1970s.*

87. **Mid-morning Break.** *Rocky Mountain Dharma Center, mid-1970s.*

88. **Afternoon Sitting, with Cat.** *Rocky Mountain Dharma Center, mid-1970s.*

89. **Night Talk in the Main Tent.** *Rocky Mountain Dharma Center, mid-1970s.*

90. **William Burroughs** (1914-1997), author of *Naked Lunch* (1959). Burroughs was invited by Trungpa and Ginsberg to give a summer writing workshop at *Naropa, 1976.*

91. **John Cage**, avant-garde composer, immediately after the premiere at Naropa of his piece *Empty Words — Part IV*. The composition included calligraphies of texts from the journals of Henry David Thoreau. John Cage "spoke" the texts by pronouncing only the consonants. Many found this disturbing. Cage's Naropa premiere happened on the day Richard Nixon resigned. At left, poet Anne Waldman. *Naropa, "Bus Terminal" building, Boulder, August 9, 1974.*

92. **Gregory Corso** (1930-2001) was the youngest member of the inner circle of original Beats with Jack Kerouac, Allen Ginsberg, and William Burroughs. Gregory Corso's books of poetry include: *The Vestal Lady and Other Poems* (1955); *Gasoline* (1958); *Bomb* (1958); *The Happy Birthday of Death* (1960); *Long Live Man* (1962); *There is Yet Time to Run Back through Life and Expiate All That's been Sadly Done* (1965); *Earth Egg* (1974); *Mind Field* (1989). At Naropa, Corso would often act the rabble-rouser and buffoon, disrupting Ginsburg's and Trungpa's talks. At one talk Trungpa threw him out. At other talks he asked, in his outrageous style, questions that truly engaged the speakers. *Naropa, 1976.*

93. **Abbie Hoffman Triumphant at a Naropa poetry slam.** Abbie Hoffman (1936-1989), activist, anarchist, and media-event-coordinator, grew up in the generation between beatniks and hippies. He co-founded the Youth International Party ("Yippees") in 1968 to protest the Vietnam war. Convicted for inciting riot against the war, he became one of "the Chicago eight." He is author of *Revolution for the Hell of it* (1968), *Woodstock Nation* (1969); *Steal This Book* (1971); and *Steal This Urine Test* (1987), among others. He participated in a poetry slam at Naropa in the summer of 1982. Behind him, the 4' x 8' painting by Karl Appel depicts Jack Kerouac with text by Allen Ginsberg, which reads "ALL YR GRAVES are O Jack of LIGHT OPEN. GUARD THE HEART. HERE'S your CROSS OF Tenderness they kept from mademoiselle." Along the bottom of the painting are the words of Jack Kerouac: "Everything belongs to me because I am poor." *Naropa, Main Building, Boulder, July 1982.*

93. **Allen Ginsberg & William Burroughs** during a sum-

mer writing workshop at *Naropa, 1975.*

94. **Robert Frank**, photographer of the highly influential work of street photography, *The Americans* (1958). *Naropa, 1975.*

95. **David Rome Reading Poetry by Trungpa.** *Naropa, mid-1970s.*

At Naropa's Nalanda campus in January 2015, for an exhibit entitled "Chögyam Trungpa Rinpoche—a Celebration of the Founding of Naropa in Photographs by Robert Del Tredici," David Rome wrote this biography of Trungpa:

A Brief Biography of Chögyam Trungpa
by David Rome

Chögyam Trungpa Rinpoche was born in 1940 into a peasant family in a remote region of eastern Tibet. At the age of 18 months he was recognized as the 11th *tulku*, or rebirth, of an important Buddhist teacher, according to the Tibetan belief that enlightened beings can return generation after generation to aid confused and suffering humans on the path to enlightenment. At an early age he was brought to Surmang, the centuries-old monastery of the Trungpa lineage, where he received a rigorous education in Buddhist doctrine and practice. At the young age of 19 he was forced to make a perilous escape across the Himalayas due to the Chinese communist invasion of Tibet and suppression of Buddhism, including the destruction of monasteries and execution of religious leaders. Trungpa's early training and escape into India in 1959 are recounted in his book *Born in Tibet.*

In 1963, with the help of a scholarship secured by Western patrons, Trungpa traveled to England to study at Oxford, the first Tibetan to do so. He immersed himself in comparative religion as well as Western philosophy and psychology. During this period he also began to teach Westerners, and in 1967 he founded Samye Ling monastery in Scotland. After renouncing his status as a monk in order to enter more fully into the world of his students, he married an English woman and, in 1970, relocated to the United States, establishing his headquarters in Boulder, Colorado.

Trungpa Rinpoche possessed an extraordinary ability to communicate the essence of Buddhist wisdom and contemplative practice in original, contemporary English language immediately accessible to the rapidly expanding numbers of his students. He was continually engaged all over North America and in Europe in giving teachings, which became the basis for numerous influential books, including *Cutting Through Spiritual Materialism*, *The Myth of Freedom*, and *Shambhala: The Sacred Path of the Warrior.* Trungpa was also an extraordinarily creative artist in many media, including poetry, theater, calligraphy, flower arranging, and photography. Trungpa Rinpoche founded the first Buddhist retreat centers in North America specifically for Western students, including Karmê-Chöling in Vermont, Shambhala Mountain Center in Colorado, and Gampo Abbey in Nova Scotia. In 1974 he founded Naropa Institute, now Naropa University, to provide a Buddhist-inspired but secular higher education rooted in contemplative wisdom. Now offering Bachelors and Masters degrees in disciplines ranging from psychology to the arts to religious studies, Naropa has become a widely known and respected academic institution.

In the 1980s Trungpa Rinpoche relocated to Nova Scotia, Canada, where he died in 1987. Today there are Shambhala meditation centers around the world, serving thousands of members, under the direction of his son Sakyong Mipham Rinpoche. Together with the Dalai Lama, Trungpa Rinpoche has been the most influential exponent of Tibetan Buddhism in the West, and a seminal figure in the current expansion of meditation and mindfulness into mainstream culture.

At the same exhibit, Naropa President Charles Lief wrote a brief biography of Trungpa Rinpoche as well. The two biographies were mounted next to each other.

Welcome From The President

Chögyam Trungpa Rinpoche: abbot, protector, lineage holder, pioneer, practitioner, scholar, professor, aesthete, painter, photographer, flower arranger, calligrapher, (a conventionally bad) singer, Tibetan-beatnik, Tibetan-Mozartian, puller of rugs, fearless shiner of spotlight on neurosis, white-tie aristocrat, khaki-clad general, snow-white adorned admiral of a landlocked navy, equestrian, magician, unconventional gourmet, unplanned friend and lover, and unexpected guru.

Naropa University, founded by Trungpa Rinpoche, came into this world as the physical manifestation of a flash of inspiration and a dream of sanity—a university cloaked in knowledge and crowned with wisdom.

Trungpa Rinpoche invited everyone to Boulder in the summer of 1974: mainstreamers and the outcasts, the artists and the academics, the students and the celebrants, all pregnant whether they knew it or not. Over the course of ten fertile weeks that summer, each gave birth in the vacated public bus storage garage on Arapahoe and Broadway where Boulder now buys its kale (several varieties, mostly organic) and drinks its coffee (fair trade).

For forty years since, Naropa faculty and students have plowed the ground, planted the seeds, contemplated and debated the difference between the flowers and the weeds, and honored the tireless effort and all-in commitment of the founder—whether they knew him or not.

Photographer Robert Del Tredici was one of the fortunate ones who bore witness to the early years, skillfully capturing the energy from the simplicity and the depth from the casual, and he has protected it all for our benefit in 2015. For that, we are grateful. Please accept our joyful invitation to enter the maze which is set out before you. Should you get lost along the way, that is your jolly good luck.

Charles G. Lief
Naropa University President

96. **Anne Waldman, poet.** In 1974 she co-founded the Jack Kerouac School of Disembodied Poetics with Allen Ginsberg, John Cage, and Diane di Prima. Today Anne is Artistic Director of the Jack Kerouac School's Naropa Summer Writing Program. From her book *Jaguar Harmonics* these verses were displayed over her portrait in the Nalanda photo exhibition of "Chögyam Trungpa Rinpoche and the Founding of Naropa" (January, 2015):

Person woven in the room, in the room to succor
    and sleep
and drink the vine

a line of men, a line of women and all between
a genderless spirit parity

and see one in the room so simple, open, you love
    him and feathered
love all the strangers tethered to the vine

97. **Under the Dream Flag** at a poetry slam with Allen Ginsberg and Chögyam Trungpa. The two poets sit in front of a graphic that Karmapa saw in a dream. Often referred to as "the dream flag," Karmapa named it *Namkhyen Gyalder* ("Victorious Flag of the Buddha's Wisdom"), saying "Wherever this banner is flown, the *Dharma* will flourish." Its blue color stands for the sky (or heaven, or wisdom, or the emptiness aspect of the awakened state); the yellow color stands for the earth (everyday experience; also compassion). The interlinked blue and yellow show the interdependence of spiritual insight and ordinary life in the *dharma*. The colored

graphic of the dream flag, below, with data on it, appears on the Dharma Haven website, *www.dharma-haven.org*. *Photo: Naropa, Main Building, 1976*.

98. **Hammer of Compassion**. Gil Figueroa setting up an event. *Boulder, late 1970s*.

99. **Warm-Up**. Barbara Dilley prepares to dance. She coordinated Naropa's Dance/Movement Studies Program and was professor of Contemporary Performance specializing in "embodied awareness"—an approach to performance that combines dance, meditation, and improvisation. She was tapped by Trungpa to serve as president of Naropa University from 1985 to 1993. *Meditation Hall and Studio, 1111 Pearl Street, Boulder, Naropa, 1975*.

100. **Regent Osel Tendzin**. Chögyam Trungpa empowered his long-time student Thomas Frederick Rich, Jr. (at the age of 33) as his Vajra Regent ("Dorje Gyaltsap") in a ceremony on August 22, 1976 in Boulder. *This photograph was taken at Karmê- Chöling in the late 1970s*.

101. **Overseeing Prajna**, a play by Chögyam Trungpa based on the *Heart Sutra*. *Naropa, Sacred Heart School, August 1974*.

102. **Prajna Rehearsal** (top). Trungpa wrote six plays: *Sand Castles* (1972); *Prajna*; *The Child of Illusion*; *Water Festival*; *Kingdom of Philosophy*; and *Proclamation* (1980). All of them were performed at Naropa. Some reveal Trungpa at his funniest. At times vaudevillian in style, they can be scandalously rude, making fun of kings, queens, gurus and others engaged in spiritual materialism. *Naropa, August, 1974*.

102. **Circle Dance** (bottom), during the Naropa premiere

of *Prajna* on August 11, 1974. The production was overseen by Trungpa, who also designed the costumes. Credit for direction went to Andrew Karr, with co-direction by Susie Niemack and Maggie Donaghy. Otto Koch was music director; costumes were made by Susie Niemack, Elaine Yuen, and Debbie Omlor. Performers in white were Lyle Weinstein, Mary Bryan, Bob Althouse, Rick Kentner, Carl Maida, Rob Curtis, and Margaret Schroeder. Performers in maroon were Erik Swanson, Alice Noaeill, Otto Koch, Poppy Koch, Maggie Donaghy, Gerry Wiener, Ruth Astor, Dana Dudley, and Elaine Yuen. Susie Niemack played Tara; Crain Smith played the Rock Man; Randy Sunday was the Fisherman.

Trungpa founded The Mudra Theatre Group to train students in drama with a series of Mudra Theatre Exercises involving Space Awareness (for body); Sound Cycles (for speech); and Gazing Exercises (for mind). The Mudra Theatre Group started soon after Trungpa designed the Maitri rooms and postures. Mudra Theatre Exercises expanded Maitri Space Awareness practices from individual meditation to theatrical performance. Play-writing and Mudra Theatre work are perhaps the least known aspects of Trungpa's teachings. *Naropa, first summer session, August, 1974*.

This is the original Prajna program, designed by Chögyam Trungpa for the play's premiere in 1974:

PRAJNA

103. **Bermuda Shorts**. Reportedly Trungpa's favorite Del Tredici photograph. *Naropa, mid-1970s.*

104. **Herding and Flocking** is the name given a dance exercise for performers searching for patterns in space and seeking ways to respond to them. Dancers begin with Follow-the-Leader moves until they notice patterns of "Herds" (shapes on the ground) or "Flocks" (forms in the air), and they become leaders, as needed, in response to the shifting patterns. The photograph depicts a Barbara Dilley rehearsal for *Following the WindHorse*, a large group dance combining native American poetry and Tibetan influences. With Marcy Vaughn (left) and Melissa Soalt (right); behind the table, with drums, is Collin Walcott. *Pearl Street Studio, Naropa, summer 1976.*

105. **Herding and Flocking (2)**. A Barbara Dilley rehearsal for *Following the WindHorse*, featuring Marcy Vaughn and Melissa Soalt, with Collin Walcott on drums; seated on floor, Sarah Keith. *Pearl Street Studio, Naropa, summer 1976.*

106. **Tai Chi** class under the direction of Jane and Bataan Faigao. *Naropa, 1977.*

107. **Parallel Corridor Map of Space** is an improvisation/composition/lecture/demonstration dance designed by Barbara Dilley to train performers to see wide and develop an eye for ensemble work. Dancer, center: Jolie Bernstein. *Naropa, 1977.*

108. ***Dancing Songs*** is a dance production by Steve Clorfeine. It premiered at 99 Prince Street in New York City under the Naropa banner. At this rehearsal in Boulder, left to right, we see Steve Clorfeine, Nancy Stark Smith, Terry O'Reilly, Rick Merrill, Cynthia Hedstrom. *Boulder, 1978.*

109. **Diagonal Improvisation**. Steve Clorfeine, supine, center. Against back wall: Steve Gorn with flute. *Naropa, 1978.*

110. **Leaning In**. Trungpa Rinpoche, in sneakers, with a *dorje* (or "*vajra*") in his right hand, suspended over his right knee, takes a question from the audience at a summer seminar. *Naropa, summer, mid-1970s.*

111. **Space Awareness Exercise** under the direction of Lee Worley. *Naropa, 1977.*

112. **Tent Awareness Exercise** with Charles Gilard. Tent culture stirs again! *Special Naropa event, late 1970s.*

113. **Tables and Chairs** with Judy Smith, Gil Figueroa (center), and Charles Gilard (right). *Naropa, late 1970s.*

Concerning tables and chairs, Chögyam Trungpa has said:

> "On the *hīnayāna* level, the teacher is a wise man. On the *mahāyāna* level, he is a physician/friend, a spiritual friend. On the *vajrayāna* level, the student-teacher relationship is similar to that in the martial arts. You could get hurt severely if you are too tense. But you could also receive a tremendous—almost physical—message. The message is not verbal or intellectual. It is like a demonstration of putting tables and chairs together. The teachings come out of the world of form, the real world of form. The teachings consist of colors and forms and sounds rather than words or ideas." ("Life of Naropa Seminar II, Talk Five, Mahamudra," in *Illusion's Game: The Life and Teachings of Naropa*).

114. **Early Naropa Graduates**. Naropa Institute was founded by Trungpa in 1974 as a nonsectarian liberal arts college promoting contemplative education. For over six years it was a candidate for accreditation from the North Central Association of Higher Education. Third person from left: Jim Jobson; fifth from left, Joe Poleo; woman next to him in front row, Sarah Kieth; then Melissa Sault; between them, one row back: Anne Zeidman; blonde man above her, Dan Montgomery; at far fight, second from the end, Jane Carpenter-Cohen. *Boulder, mid-1970s.*

115. **Early Naropa Graduation**. On the stage, left, in back row, second person: John Roper; then Barbara Dilley; then Ken Green. On Dilley's right, Regent Osel Tendzin; next to him, Sam Bercholtz; next, back row: Bob Saslov; at the end of the front row: Jeremy Hayward. On right side, front row: Bill McKeever; Reggie Ray; unidentified; Allen Ginsberg; John Barbieri. *Boulder, mid-1970s.*

116. **Visual Dharma Seminar I: 1978**. In 1978, during the week between Naropa's two summer sessions, Trungpa presented his first Visual Dharma seminar. He was responding to a request from Jack Niland and Ken Green. Jack had

been teaching Visual Dharma in the summers of 1975, 1976, and 1977. His classes filled, but he felt that Naropa administrators were not taking visual dharma seriously. Ken Green suggested they ask Trungpa himself to teach an intersession course on the topic. Trungpa accepted and expanded his role in the proceedings. In addition to giving four evening lectures that week, he organized a visual *dharma* film festival at the nearby Boulder Theatre, screening examples of Rising Sun and Setting Sun worlds. *High Noon*, *The Seven Samurai*, *Woman in the Dunes*, Orson Welles's *Othello*, *Gimmie Shelter*, and *Sunseed* were among the movies screened. There were also dharma art dances and parties. Jack designed special banners, flags, and backdrops, including an early version of the flag with the Tiger, Lion, Garuda, and Dragon—pre-Buddhist Bön icons that Trungpa imported into the world of Shambhala.

In the upper left corner of this photo we see a "four-dignities" flag (Tiger, Lion, Garuda, and Dragon were referred to as "dignities," not merely as "animals") with six large white circles on the right; the circles represent the six clans of pre-Buddhist Tibet, one of which was Trungpa's Mugpo clan. For the stage, Jack made a super-large backdrop with the four dignities to create a visual/Shambhala atmosphere for Trungpa's talks. In this photo Trungpa is explaining how the fan expresses visual dharma principles: when closed, it represents heaven; open, it represents earth; when actively moving air, it represents "man," that is, the human principle unifying heaven and earth. *Naropa, Main Building, summer 1978.*

For the Naropa exhibition at the Nalanda campus in January 2015 ("Chögyam Trungpa Rinpoche – a Celebration of the Founding of Naropa in Photographs by Robert Del Tredici"), Jack Niland wrote this statement:

The "vast vision of the Vidyahara" is a phrase we often used to try to describe the activities of Chögyam Trungpa Rinpoche. Del Tredici's photos bring back memories of that Golden Age. Trungpa was always manifesting his world, creating a down-to-earth "brick-and-mortar" kingdom where we were free to blossom. Enlightenment was a by-product in this awakened world.

Amongst the countless activities he performed was a path called Dharma Art. Here are some memories of things he said to me:

"Look deep into the space—the Magic Mirror—it contains every thing that ever was and ever will be." (1970)

"My style is a Japanese sense of space, a Tibetan use of color, and ornamentation using Western scale and materials." (1976)

"When you join Buddhism and Shambhala it creates Dharma Art. (1978)

"All there is is Dharma Art. Everything I do is Dharma Art." (1980)

"In order to change the world we must change the culture. To change the culture we must change the art. To change the art we must teach the Dharma Art principles especially to children." (1986)

117. **Open Air Sitting**. Lisa Matthews. *Naropa, late 1970s.*

118. **Construction Survey Walkabout, I**. *Karmê-Chöling, spring, 1979.*

119. **Construction Survey Walkabout, II**. *Karmê-Chöling, spring, 1979.*

120. **Boards of Eternity**. *Karmê-Chöling, 1979.*

121. **Heavy Lifting**. *Karmê-Chöling, 1979.*

122. **Ghost Boots**. At right, on the ground floor: Robin Cornman. *Karmê-Chöling, 1979.*

123. **Fire Breather**. *Karmê-Chöling, 1979.*

124. **Unveiling the Knot of Eternity**. Regent Osel Tendzin officiating. This Tibetan Buddhist symbol has also been referred to as The Endless Knot and The Knot of Meditation. It is rich in associations that include: the endless wisdom and compassion of the Buddha; phenomena locked in a closed cycle of cause-and-effect; the endless cycle of *saṃsāra*; the interweaving of time and timelessness; the union of wisdom and skillful means. Key parts of this circular wooden installation were covered in gold leaf. Karmê-Chöling's Knot of Eternity fixture was funded by a grateful John Steinbeck,

Jr., who was living there at the time to recover his health. *Karmê-Chöling, late 1970s.*

125. **Raising Dharma Flags.** *Karmê-Chöling.*

126. **Interview.** *Karmê-Chöling, late 1970s.*

127. **Samadhi Cushions, Inc.**, was founded at Karmê-Chöling in 1976 by Irv and Jeanine Weiner. Its main products are hand-made meditation cushions (*zafus*), hand-made yoga mats (*zabutons*), and kneeling meditation benches made from wood grown in Vermont. Samadhi Cushions is still making meditation items today. On left: John Odenthal. *Karmê-Chöling, mid-1970s.*

128. **Sitting Under Ceiling Under Construction.** *Karmê-Chöling, late 1970s.*

129. **Post-meditation.** *Zafus* by Samadhi Cushions. *Karmê-Chöling, late 1970s.*

130. **Woman at a Window.** *Karmê-Chöling, late 1970s.*

131. **Mother and Child.** *Karmê-Chöling.*

132. **Wedding Play.** *Karmê-Chöling, mid-1970s.*

133. **La Pointessa.** *Karmê-Chöling, mid-1970s.*

134. **Table Talk.** *Karmê-Chöling, early 1970s.*

135. **Two Humans, Grounded, Looking Up.** *Karmê-Chöling, early 1970s.*

136. **Dorje Root with Diana and Chögyam's son Gesar Mugpo.** *Karmê-Chöling, 1973.*

137. **Mother and Child,** also Frank Berliner (far right). *Karmê-Chöling, mid-1970s.*

138. **Leaning & Reading** while *sangha* members prepare for a special event at *Karmê-Chöling, late 1970s.*

139. **In Anticipation.** Gary Hubiak on his wedding day. *Karmê-Chöling, mid-1970s.*

141. **Ritual Galyang Horns** herald Karmapa's presence. Fourth monk down the line: Rumtek Chant Master Umdze Thupten. Fifth monk: Jomgon Kongtrul. During Karmapa's second visit to the West. *Karmê-Chöling, 1976.*

142. **Shambhala Day Feast with Karmapa.** On left, first person: Michael McClellan; second person, looking at camera: Dr. Mitchell Levy; fourth person: Gary Hubiak. On right side, second person: Suzanne Janowitz; third: Frank Berliner; fourth: Barbara Mann Smith; sixth: Bill McKeever, speaking with Achi Tsepal, Karmapa's translator. In back, far right:

John Odenthal. During Karmapa's second visit to the West, he visited Vermont, Boston, New York City, Boulder, Chicago, Los Angeles, and San Francisco. *Karmê-Chöling, 1976.*

143. **Strolling Through Burlington** during Karmapa's second visit. On Karmapa's left, Michael McClellan; next to him, Jomgon Kongtrul; then monk Tsultim. *Burlington, Vermont, 1976.*

144. **Karmapa Descending a Staircase.** At Karmapa's side, Michael McClellan. Monk in front: Rumtek Chant Master Umdze Thupten. *Burlington Mall, Burlington, Vermont, 1976.*

145. **Karmapa Passing Manikin,** with Michael McClellan. *Burlington Mall, Burlington, Vermont, 1976.*

146. **Karmapa Studies Suspended Column of Ornate Pillows.** Behind Karmapa, Michael McClellan. Monk at far left: Rumtek Chant Master Umdze Thupten. At far right, in fur coat: Olive Colon. *Burlington Mall, Burlington, Vermont, 1976.*

147. **The Contemplation of Purses.** *Burlington Mall, Burlington, Vermont, 1976.*

148. **Browsing.** *Burlington Mall, Burlington, Vermont, 1976.*

149. **Window Portrait.** Far left: Michael McClellan. *Burlington Mall, Burlington, Vermont, 1976.*

150. **Biding Time at the Burlington TV Station.** The Sanskrit on the banner says *evam*, or "thus." It is the personal seal of the Trungpa *tulkus.* *Burlington Mall, Burlington, Vermont, 1976.*

151. **Achi Points the Way.** The Burlington TV station produced a program featuring Karmapa, his monks, and Jomgon Kongtrul III; it was at one time available at the site with the address: *karmapa.900.org/Karmapa.16th.html Burlington TV station, 1976.*

152. **Karmapa with the Mayor of Montreal Jean Drapeau,** who held the office for three decades (1954-1957; 1960-1986) and was responsible for the Montreal subway system, the Place des Arts concert hall; Expo 67; and the 1976 summer Olympics. *Office of the Mayor, Montreal City Hall, May, 1977.*

153. **Jomgon Kongtrul Contemplating a Model of Montreal's Olympic Stadium.** The Olympic Stadium ("the Big O", sometimes referred to as "the Big Owe"), was designed

by French architect Roger Taillibert. There were problems with the retractable roof; the stadium was not completed until three decades after the Olympics ended. It plunged the City of Montreal into a debt of $1.61 billion. *Office of the Mayor, Montreal City Hall, May, 1977.*

154. Photo opportunity on the front steps of City Hall. *Office of the Mayor, Montreal City Hall, May, 1977.*

155. Spritz. *Karmê-Chöling, 1976.*

156. Reeds with Monk at the Maitri Center during Karmapa's visit there. *Wingdale, New York. 1976.*

157. Holy Breeze. Karmapa on his visit to the Maitri Center. *Wingdale, New York, 1976.*

159. The Hills are Alive with Karmapa/von Trapp. In the foreground, translator Achi Tsepal. In the center, Jomgon Kongtrul III. At far left, Baroness Maria Augusta Kutschera von Trapp (1905-1987), matroness of the Trapp Family Singers, here at age 71. The Trapp family moved from Europe to a farmhouse in Stowe, Vermont in the 1940s. In 1943 the farmhouse collapsed under the Vermont winter snow. The family rebuilt, and Maria named their new lodge *Cor Unum* ("One Heart"). *Trapp Family Lodge ("Cor Unum"), Stowe, Vermont, December, 1976.*

160. Karmapa Triptych:
Image One: Prayerful.
Image Two: Upward Gaze.

161. Karmapa Triptych:
Image Three: Quizzical. *Trapp Family Lodge ("Cor Unum"), Stowe, Vermont. December 1976.*

162. Lohan Reflecting. *Shrine Room, Karmê-Chöling, 1975.*

163. Gargoylesque. *Karmê-Chöling, 1976.*

164. Afternoon Nap. Older Lama, left: Rumtek Chant Master Umdze Thupten. Sleeping monk: the brother of Ponlop Rinpoche. *Near Lake Champlain, Lachute, Quebec, May, 1977.*

165. Il Penseroso. Lama Gigme. *Karmê-Chöling, 1977.*

166. The Way of the Canoe. In front, Tsultim Namgyal; in back, the Third Bardor Tulku Rinpoche. Bardor Tulku trained as a *tulku* under Karmapa XVI. He helped establish Karmapa's seat in the west, Karma Triyana Dharmachakra. In 2003 he es-tablished the Tibetan Buddhist center, Kenzang Palchen Ling, in Red Hook, New York, where he currently teaches. *Lake Champlain, Lachute, Quebec, May, 1977.*

167. High Noon. Karmapa makes his move. At left, Achi the translator. *Beverly Webster's chalet on Lake Champlain, Lachute, Quebec, May, 1977.*

168. Jomgon Kongtrul with Cape in front of Beverly Webster's chalet. *Lake Champlain, Lachute , Quebec, May, 1977.*

169. Jomgon Kongtrul Up Close. *Trapp Family Lodge, Cor Unum, Stowe, Vermont, December, 1976.*

170. Jomgon Kongtrul Preparing to Speak. *Karmê-Chöling, 1977.*

171. Jomgon Kongtrul Under Solar Flare. The Very Venerable Jomgon Kongtrul III, Rinpoche, was one of the four main disciples (or "princes") of the Gyalwa Karmapa. Fifteen years later, on April 22, 1992, at the age of 37, he died in a car crash in Darjeeling. *Lake Champlain, Lachute, Quebec, May, 1977.*

172. Spiegel in Suit with Bell-Bottoms. Karmapa's visit in 1974 prompted Trungpa to establish a *sangha* dress code: suits and ties for men; blouses and knee-length skirts for women. Eric Spiegel bought his suits at Fashion Bar in the Crossroads Shopping Center in Boulder. *Vajra Assembly, Karmê-Chöling, August, 1978.* See also page 63.

173. Playing Galyang Horns during Karmapa's visit to the Montreal Dharmadhatu. Monk on left: Rumtek Chant Master Umdze Thupten. *Montreal, May, 1977.*

174. The Iron Path. *Karmê-Chöling, 1977.*

175. Reclining Onlooker. Don Doneghy, photographer. *Naropa, Sacred Heart School, mid-1970s.*

176. Assembling the Throne for the Karmapa. *Karmê-Chöling, 1977.*

177. The Black Crown Ceremony has been designed to benefit all sentient beings. Karmapa performed the Black Crown many times during his visits to the West. The ceremony originated with the 5th Karmapa, Dezhin Shegpa (1384-1415). The Black Crown, also referred to as the Vajra Crown, symbolizes the power-field of wisdom-energy present in each of the Karmapas; it is said to sometimes manifest in nonmaterial form above the Karmapa's head. In the photo, the ceremony has just been completed, and the crown has been returned to its storage box at the far right. The child in foreground, at left, is Ariella, held by her mother Clare Futral. *Karmê-Chöling, 1974.*

178. **Ascent.** Jomgon Kongtrul III at *Karmê-Chöling, 1977.*

179. **Descent.** Karmapa with Lama Jigme. *Karmê-Chöling, winter, 1977.*

180. **Monks with Horses (top).** Left: The Third Bardor Tulku Rinpoche. *Stowe, Vermont, December, 1976.*

180. **Holy Paparazzi (bottom).** Between the monks: Michael Chender. *Karmê-Chöling, December, 1977.*

181. **Camera Shy.** Lama Jigme awaits the appearance of Karmapa. *Karmê-Chöling, December, 1977.*

183. **Group Portrait with Karmapa** taken near the end of Karmapa's second visit to Karmê-Chöling. Identified in the photo so far: Michael McClellan, Frank Berliner, Olive Colon, Irv Wei, Mark Spikowski, Cathy Hubiak, Karmê-Chöling Architect Richard Rice, Jeannie Weider, Suzanne Brock, Bill McKeever, Jan Watson; Karmapa, Jomgon Kongtrul III, Lama Jigme, Tagi, Achi Tsepal, Lama Lodro Sherab, Lama Thupten Lamze, Tsultim Namgyal, Rumtek Chant Master Umdze Thupten. *Karmê-Chöling, December 21, 1977.*

185. **Flower Moon.** Trungpa at work on his first Ikebana show, in Denver's oldest church, a stone Romanesque/Gothic chapel named Emmanuel, dedicated in 1876 to serve an Episcopalian congregation; in 1903 it was converted to a Jewish synagogue; from 1959 to 1973 it became an arts studio. In 1969 it was listed as a historic place in the National Register of Historic Places. Now called The Emmanuel Gallery, it is located on the Auraria Campus in downtown Denver. The Gallery is shared by the University of Colorado in Denver, Metro State College, and the Community College of Denver. *July, 1978.*

186. **Ikebana Mountain Salute.** The Explorers of the Richness of the Phenomenal World, a group founded by Trungpa, meet in the foothills of the Rockies to gather materials for one of Trungpa's large-scale *ikebana* installations. Left to right: unknown; Trungpa; Ludwick Turzanski, Head Explorer; Nick Wright; Richard Pelsinger; Marcia Wang-Shibata. *In the foothills of the Rockies outside Boulder, 1978.*

Ludwick Turzanski's statement, below, was included in the exhibit "Chögyam Trungpa Rinpoche – a Celebration of the Founding of Naropa in Photographs by Robert Del Tredici" at Naropa's Nalanda campus, January 28-April 12, 2015.

The experience of working with Trungpa Rinpoche on flower arranging and Dharma Art still arises vividly in my mind and heart. When Rinpoche first arrived in the mountains of Boulder in 1970, I was a newly minted professor of art, and we discovered that we both admired the Japanese aesthetic.

Soon after Rinpoche settled into a house in Four Mile Canyon he invited me to help him with an Ikebana arrangement. He described the flowers and greenery he wanted and what he needed the main branch to look like. I loved traipsing over the hills and through the woods looking for precisely the right branch to appear. I was to serve Rinpoche in this capacity, joyfully, for the rest of his life.

Over time Rinpoche's arrangements grew larger, and they were shared more publicly. He made his first big arrangement for a show with my sculpture class at the Henderson Museum Gallery on the Boulder campus of the University of Colorado in 1973.

In 1975 Rinpoche was invited to exhibit at the Emmanuel Gallery on the Denver campus of the University of Colorado. This became the first of his "environmental installations," which Rinpoche was to do more times in Boulder, Denver, Los Angeles, and San Francisco. The "environmental" aspect of these shows meant that the whole gallery became a unique space which the flower arrangements articulated. In time the concept was formalized to encompass an entrance room, a kitchen, a study, an audience hall, a Buddha room, a warrior room, and, in Los Angeles, at the end, a drum room.

It soon became clear that one or two assistants would no longer be sufficient. Rinpoche asked me to put together a group of helpers we would call "The Explorers of the Richness of the Phenomenal World." The name expresses the simple truth that our world is inherently rich if we open to it with a fresh mind. "Art" is simply an expression of that.

Ernie Porps was my second in command, and Gabrielle Bershen, Carol Halpern, and James Hoagland were Explorer "regulars" in Boulder who worked with me on most of the exhibits. Other Explorers were Marcia Shibata, Paula Breymier, David Wright, Rachel Homer, Peter DiGesu, Michael and Eve Reshetnik, Joel Simon, Linda Ellis, and Kimiko Snyder. There were also helpers outside Boulder who pitched in when one of Trungpa Rinpoche's exhibits was held in their town.

As "Head Explorer" I organized people into departments and teams. We experimented making mats, containers, and unique branch-holders in many sizes. We researched rocks, branches, flower sources, and vases. After months of planning, a framework emerged which would provide the skillful means needed to make this and subsequent shows happen. The work was demanding and grandly adventurous.

We didn't stop there. Rinpoche and I came up with the idea to have the Explorers become a sort of dharmic "Outward Bound" group which would combine mindfulness with an understanding of the subtleties of the natural environment. People would learn to scale rocks, climb trees, recognize flowers and plants, understand the movement of birds and the flow of streams, and read the weather in skies and clouds. Rinpoche particularly liked the idea of learning survival skills that did not rely on killing any animals. For a variety of reasons, the most important being Rinpoche's declining health, these ideas were never fully realized. But there is always the possibility that this aspect of Rinpoche's vast and playful vision will yet find fruition in the future.

Ludwick Turzanski

187. **Choosing Elbow Pine**. Next to the tree: Marcia Wang-Shibata; Ludwick Turzanski; Charles Gilard. *In the foothills of the Rockies outside Boulder, 1978.*

188. **Reaching High**. Trungpa at work on his first public Ikebana display. *Emmanuel Gallery, Auraria Campus, Denver, July 1978.*

189. **Kudos All Around**. Trungpa completes his first Ikebana exhibition. *Emmanuel Gallery, Auraria Campus, July 1978.*

190. **Ikebana Charnel Ground**. With Ludwick Turzanski. *Boulder Community Center, late 1970s.*

191. **Ikebana Consult** with Ludwick Turzanski and Marcia Wang-Shibata. In back: Judy Smith (left); Adona Barbieri (center, pointing); Jim Stinson (right). *Boulder, 1978.*

Marcia Wang-Shibata's statement, below, was part of the exhibit "Chögyam Trungpa Rinpoche – a Celebration of the Founding of Naropa in Photographs by Robert Del Tredici" at the Nalanda campus of Naropa, January-April 2015.

Ikebana and the Vidyadhara

It wasn't particularly pleasant to be with him; actually it was kind of awful most of the time because you never knew what was going to happen next. I don't think he did either, but he never turned away from anyone or any situation as useless or undesirable. In flower arrangement and in everything else, he taught us this: ⊠there is always the right place and time for everything, there is no such thing as waste …

He didn't really arrange anything. He just added something or took something away in relationship to what was already there, step by step.

His most profound arrangement was one flower in a vase with no leaves.

I told him once that he was not following the rules. He just looked at me and grinned.

His flower arrangements were probably his best teachings. There was no talking, no discussion, nothing to "teach". They were just clear and direct, dignified, simple and complete by themselves, the way he was, vast and ordinary at the same time, and always a little bit strange somehow.

He always related to us from the wisdom in space, just the way all the trees, plants, and flowers are constantly nourished and have remained compatible with each other forever, long before we humans arrived.

He never really taught us much about Ikebana⬚ or anything else for that matter. He just gave us the bones, then we had to discover the muscles and skin and bring life blood to it all.

His flower arrangements weren't very Japanese at all, nor were they very Tibetan in style. They were just distilled expressions of nature with both her beauty and terror, like you and I.

He was always very kind to me.

Marcia Wang-Shibata

192. **Abuzz Over New Ikebana**. At right, in front of white rectangle: Penny Lindsay; to the right: Ludwick Turzanski. Trungpa spoke for four evenings in the week of his first Visual Dharma Seminar. *Naropa, 1978.*

193. **Visual Dharma Seminar I, 1978: Night Four**. In the week between Naropa's two summer sessions, Trungpa gave his first Visual Dharma seminar. He spoke on four evenings. The first evening he gave a slideshow on the history of art,

showing how the principles of Heaven, Earth, and Man had been intuitively grasped by many artists. The second evening he made calligraphies on an opaque projector to demonstrate visual dharma principles. In his third lecture he showed how visual dharma can be expressed in object arrangements. In his final presentation he discussed visual dharma in relation to the art of Ikebana.

Jack Niland's banner on the far left was an early visualization of the Great Eastern Sun. Jack's giant backdrop behind Trungpa depicts, going counter-clockwise, Tiger (orange), Lion (white), Garuda (red), and Dragon (blue). Jack went on to make many banners with these four iconic creatures; but he created only one giant backdrop—for the Visual Dharma seminar. *Naropa, Main Building, summer, 1978.*

194. **Line of Sight**. Trungpa checks out Marc Diamond's large format camera. *Boulder, 1978.*

195. **Jeanne Perks on her Wedding Night**. Carolyn Gimian is doing Jeanne's hair. *Boulder, June 1, 1976.*

196. **Donna Sunday and Sakyong Mipham** at the Perks wedding party. *Judy Smith's house, Boulder, June 1, 1976.*

197. **Elizabeth Pybus**, mother of Diana. *Boulder, late 1970s.*

198. **The Arch of Steel**. Jeanne and John get married. Part of the ceremony included passing under an arch of swords. According to John Perks, this represents a safe transition to a new life making two into one. Many people called John Perks "Trungpa's butler;" he prefers to be referred to as "Rinpoche's servant or attendant." *Judy Smith's house, Boulder, June 1, 1976.*

199. **Trungpa Toasts the Perks** at their wedding party. At left, Tom Rykin. According to John Perks, Trungpa's white uniform was purchased at Geives and Hawkes on Saville Row in London. Trungpa bought several uniforms there. Geives and Hawkes kept Trungpa's measurements on file under the name Mr. Mugpo. *Judy Smith's house, Boulder, June 1, 1976.*

200. **John Perks Raises a Glass** at his wedding party. In the center, raising her glass higher: Cindy Guest. Perks' uniform, like Trungpa's, was acquired at Geives and Hawkes on Saville Row. *Judy Smith's house, Boulder, June 1, 1976.*

201. **Party Mix**. Right of center, bending, Dana Marshall.

On her right: Dana's father George Marshall. Perks wedding party, *Judy Smith's house, Boulder, June 1, 1976.*

202. **Hanging Out.** On Trungpa's right, the Regent; at Trungpa's left, Cindy Guest. *Judy Smith's house, Boulder, June 1, 1976.*

203. **Party Talk** at the Perks wedding party. *Judy Smith's house, Boulder, June 1, 1976.*

205. **Ride of the Valkyries.** Golf cart, left, driven by Terry Tighe; cart at right driven by Sakyong Mipham with Jim Stinson on his right. *Lake Valley Golf Course, Boulder, late 1970s.*

206. **Dharma Handshake.** Trungpa and the Regent. *Lake Valley Golf Course, Boulder, late 1970s.*

207. **Teeing Off.** *Lake Valley Golf Course, Boulder, late 1970s.*

209. **Big Golf.** Far left: Valerie Williams; Trungpa; Tery Tighe (in dark glasses); Jim Stinson; the Regent; Myron Simms; Nicholas Esposet; Cathy Kaiser. *Lake Valley Golf Course, Boulder, late 1970s.*

210. **Vidyadhara with Video.** *Lake Valley Golf Course, Boulder, late 1970s.*

211. **Regent in the Distance.** *Lake Valley Golf Course, Boulder, late 1970s.*

212. **On the Green.** *Lake Valley Golf Course, Boulder, late 1970s.*

213. **Sakyong Mipham with Mastiff of Trungpa, Ganesh.** Trungpa empowered Osel Rangdro Mukpo (Sakyong Mipham) as his successor and dharma heir in 1979. *Boulder, late 1970s.*

215. **Turning the Wheel in Manhattan.** In second row: Irv and Jeanine Weiner, founders of Samadhi Cushions at Tail of the Tiger; second row, next to Jeanine, Lee Wingrad. Perhaps Alan Ginsberg standing against the far white wall. On his right, perhaps Lama Ugyen. Craig Smith and George Marshall are in the audience. The two banners flanking the central *evam* symbol bear the Maitri logos. *New York City, early 1970s.*

214. **Hearing the Dharma.** The sound-recording technician's task is to insure that people in the future will have access to Trungpa Rinpoche's talks. *Naropa, mid-1970s.*

217. **Vajra Slash.** With Carol Halpern. *Boulder, early 1980s.*

218. **Cat-Tails** with Max King, who was sometimes referred to as "cookie divine" for his culinary aplomb as one of Trungpa's chefs. Windswept Spruce installation. *Boulder Center for the Visual Arts, now Boulder Museum of Contemporary Art (BMoCA), 1978-1981.*

219. **Dark Flowers.** Far right, Max King; near him, Carol Halpern. Windswept Spruce installation. *Boulder Center for the Visual Arts (now BMoCA), 1978-81.*

220. **Pine Alert** with Monk Tsultim. Windswept Spruce. *Boulder Center for the Visual Arts (now BMoCA), 1978-81.*

221. **Exploding Ikebana** with monk Tsultim. Windswept Spruce. *Boulder Center for the Visual Arts (now BMoCA), 1978-81.*

222 & 223. **Iwo Jima Double Feature with Two Trungpas.** Tree on right (Carol Halpern in background) visually flows into tree on left (with Ron Barnstone, far right; in middle: Gabrielle Bershen). Windswept Spruce. *Boulder Center for the Visual Arts (now BMoCA), 1978-81.*

224. **Cosmic Mirror.** Windswept Spruce. *Boulder Center for the Visual Arts (now BMoCA), 1978-81.*

225. **In the Moment.** *Boulder Center for the Visual Arts (now BMoCA), 1978-81.*

226. **Standing Ikebana.** *Boulder Center for the Visual Arts (now BMoCA), 1978-81.*

227. **Sitting Ikebana.** In back, head in front of window: Max King; woman raising arms: Gabrielle Berchon. *Boulder Center for the Visual Arts (now BMoCA), 1978-81.*

228. **Ikebana Sunyata** with Carol Halpern. *Boulder Center for the Visual Arts (now BMoCA), 1978-81.*

229. **Distant Guru.** With Ron Barnstone and Carol Halpern. *Boulder Center for the Visual Arts (now BMoCA), 1978-81.*

230. **Room with Pine.** *Boulder Center for the Visual Arts (now BMoCA), 1978-81.*

231. **Ikebana Under Construction.** *Naropa, 1979.*

232. **Big Fabric** with monk Tsultim and Ludwick Turzanski. *Boulder Center for the Visual Arts (now BMoCA), 1978-81.*

233. **Ikebana Assistant.** *Boulder Center for the Visual Arts (now BMoCA), 1978-81.*

234. **Waterfall**. Monk Tsultim on ladder. *Boulder Center for the Visual Arts (now BMoCA), 1978-81.*

235. **With Lady Diana**. Exhibition opening for the Windswept Spruce installation. *Boulder Center for the Visual Arts (now BMoCA), 1978-81.*

237. **Flower Demon**. Trungpa makes tracks while setting up Windswept Spruce. *Boulder Center for the Visual Arts (now BMoCA), 1978-81.*

238. **Contemplating Trungpa Ikebanas**. *Boulder Center for the Visual Arts (now BMoCA), 1978-81.*

239. **Safari**. Windswept Spruce installation. *Boulder Center for the Visual Arts (now BMoCA), 1978-81.*

241. **Visual Dharma Seminar 1: 1978** Trungpa at the 1978 Naropa summer Visual Dharma seminar demonstrating visual *dharma* principles through the art of calligraphy. *Naropa, summer, 1979.*

242. **Visual Dharma Seminar 2: 1979**. Trungpa followed up his 1978 summer intersession Visual Dharma seminar with a 1979 summer intersession Visual Dharma seminar. At this talk, the topic was visual dharma expressed through calligraphy. *Naropa, summer, 1979.*

244. **Circle in the Square: Manifesting Peace (top)**. Visual Dharma Seminar 2. *Naropa, summer, 1979.*

244. **Triangle in the Square: Manifesting Action (bottom)**. Visual Dharma Seminar 2. *Naropa, summer, 1979.*

243. **Square In the Square: Manifesting Enriching**. Visual Dharma Seminar 2. *Naropa, summer, 1979.*

245. **All Five Buddha Family Energies Together**. Visual Dharma Seminar 2. *Naropa, summer, 1979.*

247. **Drala Mounted**. *Riding Stable, North Boulder, summer, 1982.*

249. **Riding Drala**. *North Boulder, summer, 1982.*

251. **After the Ride**. *Riding Stable, North Boulder, summer, 1982.*

253. **Portrait with Drala**. My last photograph of Chögyam Trungpa. *Riding Stable, North Boulder, summer, 1982.*

Printed in the USA
CPSIA information can be obtained
at www.ICGtesting.com
LVHW070240181023
761435LV00011B/57